#movements

#NeverAgain

Preventing Gun Violence

Rachael L. Thomas

Abdo & Daughters

An Imprint of Abdo Publishing
abdobooks.com

abdobooks.com

Published by Abdo Publishing, a division of ABDO, PO Box 398166, Minneapolis, Minnesota 55439. Copyright © 2020 by Abdo Consulting Group, Inc. International copyrights reserved in all countries. No part of this book may be reproduced in any form without written permission from the publisher. Abdo & Daughters™ is a trademark and logo of Abdo Publishing.

Printed in the United States of America, North Mankato, Minnesota
052019
092019

Design: Aruna Rangarajan, Mighty Media, Inc.
Production: Mighty Media, Inc.
Editor: Liz Salzmann
Cover Photographs: Shutterstock
Interior Photographs: Design elements, Shutterstock; AP Images, pp. 11, 15, 18–19, 23, 24–25; Getty Images, pp. 8–9; Lorie Shaull/Wikimedia Commons, p. 5; North Wind Picture Archives, p. 7; Shutterstock, pp. 3, 12–13, 16–17, 20, 26–27, 28 (top), 28 (bottom left), 28 (bottom right), 29 (bottom), 29 (top right), 29 (top left)

Library of Congress Control Number: 2018966469

Publisher's Cataloging-in-Publication Data
Names: Thomas, Rachael L., author.
Title: #NeverAgain: Preventing Gun Violence / by Rachael L. Thomas
Other title: Preventing gun violence
Description: Minneapolis, Minnesota : Abdo Publishing, 2020 | Series: #Movements | Includes online resources and index.
Identifiers: ISBN 9781532119323 (lib. bdg.) | ISBN 9781532173783 (ebook)
Subjects: LCSH: Firearms ownership--Juvenile literature. | Gun control--United States--Juvenile literature. | Gun control--Law and legislation--Juvenile literature. | Protest movements--Juvenile literature.
Classification: DDC 323--dc23

CONTENTS

It was February 14, 2018, at Marjory Stoneman Douglas High School in Parkland, Florida. Students were attending classes and exchanging valentines. But this scene would soon be torn apart by tragedy.

A little after 2:00 p.m., former student Nikolas Cruz entered the school and began shooting an automatic rifle. Students and teachers tried to protect themselves and others. The building was evacuated.

Police later arrested Cruz. But it was too late for the victims of his attack. Fourteen students, two coaches, and a teacher were killed.

Students at Marjory Stoneman Douglas High School were angered by the attack. If gun control laws were stricter, they argued, Nikolas Cruz might not have been able to kill innocent people. A small group of students turned to social media to take action. They declared that the events of February 14 should never again be allowed to happen. With the hashtag #NeverAgain, the debate on gun control was launched with more passion than ever before.

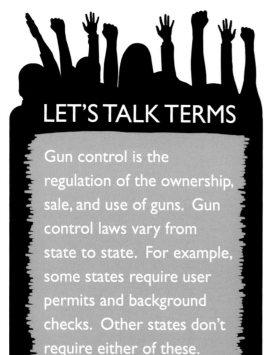

LET'S TALK TERMS

Gun control is the regulation of the ownership, sale, and use of guns. Gun control laws vary from state to state. For example, some states require user permits and background checks. Other states don't require either of these.

The US represents only 4.4 percent of the world's population. But almost half of all civilian-owned guns in the world are in the US.

The history of gun ownership in the US dates back to colonial times. During this period, local militias defended towns from attack by British soldiers and other threats. Lawmakers wanted militias to be able to protect themselves and their country. So in 1791, the right to keep and bear arms was added to the US Constitution. This right became the Second Amendment.

To this day, guns have a unique place in US history and culture. Many Americans see gun ownership as a part of the national identity and a way of life. But other Americans argue this way of life has led to high rates of gun crime.

At various points in US history, dramatic events involving guns have made people push for stricter gun control. One of these was the assassination of President John F. Kennedy in November 1963. In April 1968, civil rights activist Martin Luther King Jr. was also assassinated. In response to these killings, Congress passed the Gun Control Act (GCA) later in 1968. One requirement included in the GCA was that every manufactured gun had to have its own serial number. This allowed guns to be tracked and monitored.

In March 1981, another gunman tried to kill President Ronald Reagan. The gunman shot Reagan, a secret service agent, and Press Secretary James

The first guns were brought to the Americas by European explorers and colonists.

James Brady (*left*) was present when President Bill Clinton (*right*) signed the Brady Act.

Brady. All three recovered. However, Brady became permanently disabled from the attack.

After the shooting, Brady campaigned passionately for stricter gun control. Finally, in 1993, the Brady Handgun Violence Prevention Act was passed. The act established the National Instant Criminal Background Check System. This system checks whether someone has been convicted of certain types of crimes before allowing him or her to buy a gun.

The past 20 years have seen a rise in another type of gun violence. This is mass shootings at schools. In 1999, two students at a Colorado high school shot and killed 12 students and a teacher. In 2007, a student shot and killed 32 people on a Virginia college campus. And in 2012, a young man shot and killed 20 children and six staff members at an elementary school in Connecticut.

These and other school shootings brought the issue of gun control to national attention. Many people called for stricter gun control laws to prevent future shootings. Others thought better security in schools was the answer. Eventually, public attention would turn to a new issue, and the debate on gun control would subside.

The Parkland shooting defied this trend. Its young survivors did not allow the shooting to be forgotten. When the hashtag #NeverAgain launched, its creators were fighting for real policy change. And they were not willing to back down.

Many of the students at Marjory Stoneman Douglas High School felt traumatized after the Parkland shooting. Some had seen their friends and teachers killed. Others had fled or hidden in terror until the attack was over. The community was in mourning.

Cameron Kasky was an 11th-grader who survived the Parkland shooting. Kasky wanted to do more than quietly grieve. He wanted change. The day after the shooting, he invited fellow students Alex Wind and Jaclyn Corin to his house. Together, they created the hashtag #NeverAgain.

Kasky gathered more students to work on the campaign. He, Corin, and Wind were soon joined by Emma González and David Hogg. These five students would become the leaders of the #NeverAgain movement.

TAGGED

"When I started organizing this trip to Tallahassee, I had no idea if any of my classmates would even want to go. Now the world is watching..."

—Jaclyn Corin
(@JaclynCorin, Twitter)

The #NeverAgain team created digital content about gun control as part of their campaign. This included videos, social media posts, and memes. This content attracted a huge following. For example, González did not have a Twitter account before the attack. She created an account to tweet about the #NeverAgain campaign. One month after the attack, González had more than one million followers!

Survivors of the Parkland shooting meet with President Trump at the White House.

The small team of student survivors worked quickly. The Parkland shooting had attracted lots of media attention. Being in the national spotlight was valuable. It made it easier for the Parkland survivors to be seen and heard across the nation. Within days, the team had arranged for a group of students to travel to Tallahassee, the Florida state capital. There, they spoke with the state's lawmakers about gun control.

Meanwhile, the #NeverAgain movement continued to gain media attention. On February 21, President Donald Trump met with a group of students, parents, and teachers who were affected by the shootings at Parkland and other schools. Trump listened to their accounts of the shootings and discussed possible solutions. Shortly after, the five #NeverAgain leaders were interviewed by CBS. The interview was featured in an episode of *60 Minutes*, which aired on March 18, 2018.

David Hogg is

the primary media face of the movement. Hogg had worked at his school's TV station. He later co-wrote a book about the attack and movement with his sister, a fellow Parkland student.

Emma González

is the public speaker of the group. She was interviewed by several news stations after the attack. She also made a powerful speech at the March for Our Lives event in Washington, DC. She created an iconic moment onstage when she stood in silence to mark how long the shooting lasted.

ONLINE ACTIVISM

The Parkland students are considered "digital natives." This means they grew up using computers and social media. After the Parkland shooting, social media became just as important as mainstream media. It represented a new, online form of protest.

THE FACES OF #NEVERAGAIN

Cameron Kasky

was the one who first rallied students to his home to organize the movement's efforts. He also became known for a televised town hall event held by Florida Senator Marco Rubio. During the event, Kasky challenged Rubio's acceptance of National Rifle Association (NRA) campaign donations.

Alex Wind is a key

coordinator of efforts that involve students and organizations from other states across the US.

Jaclyn Corin does

most of the planning for the group. She organized the initial trip to Tallahassee for 100 classmates to challenge Florida's state lawmakers.

The Parkland shooting was front-page news for longer than any other mass shooting to date. While Parkland students worked to maintain media attention, they were also organizing a large-scale street protest. The event was called March for Our Lives. It took place on March 24, 2018, in Washington, DC.

Hundreds of thousands of people attended the march in Washington. It was an event that aimed to involve mostly young people. So, #NeverAgain activists decided that only young people would address the crowd. Speakers included 17-year-old Edna Chavez and 11-year-old Christopher Underwood. Both of them had lost their brothers to gun violence.

González also made a powerful speech. She spoke briefly about how the Parkland shooting had affected the community. Then she stood silently until a timer she had brought with her beeped. She explained that the timer went off six minutes and twenty seconds after she took the stage. This was how long the Parkland shooting had lasted.

TAGGED

"Good Morning! It's a beautiful day to remember that teachers shouldn't have to worry about anything except their Home Life and Educating their Students (and maybe sometimes planning ice cream parties but thats just me)"
—Emma González
(@Emma4Change, Twitter)

During González's silence, the crowd cheered her name and chanted, "Never again!"

One goal of March for Our Lives was to encourage young people to vote. The voter-registration group HeadCount sent volunteers to US marches to sign up young voters.

Beyond Washington, hundreds of other cities hosted smaller protests under the March for Our Lives banner. In all, 763 marches in support of gun control were held in the US on March 24, 2018. Protesters in Alaska marched even though it was −25 degrees Fahrenheit (−32°C) outside!

Officials have estimated that the combined attendance for all US marches was between 1.3 and 2.2 million. But this doesn't include marches outside the US. Another 84 marches were held in other countries across the world.

Such a big event involved much planning and organization. But the #NeverAgain activists had help. The Women's March of January 2017 had brought almost 500,000 people to the streets of Washington. So, Women's March organizer Deena Katz offered her experience to help Parkland students plan the March for Our Lives.

#NeverAgain also received large donations from supporters. Celebrities, including George and Amal Clooney, donated to the cause. The team also used the fundraising website GoFundMe to raise money. Through GoFundMe, they raised more than $4 million. Support for the #NeverAgain movement was booming.

The Parkland activists planned to use donations to help meet their objectives. The most important objective of the movement was changing policies on gun control. Several changes were successfully made soon after the shooting.

On March 9, 2018, Florida Governor Rick Scott signed a new bill. This bill raised the minimum age to buy a gun from 18 to 21. It also imposed a three-day waiting period on gun sales for most buyers. This means a gun buyer has to wait at least three days after paying for a gun to actually receive it. During this time, a background check on the buyer is conducted. Finally, the bill banned bump stocks. A bump stock is an attachment that allows a rifle to fire bullets almost as fast as a machine gun. This attachment makes the weapon much deadlier.

Governor Scott's bill was an achievement for the Parkland survivors. But it only applied to the state of Florida. To change policy across all US states, federal law must be changed.

The Parkland gunman used a Smith & Wesson M&P15 rifle, which is one brand of AR-15. This type of weapon was also used in several other mass shootings, including the one at Sandy Hook.

Shortly after the Parkland shooting, a group of teenagers staged a "lie-in" outside the White House to show support for stricter gun control laws.

On March 23, President Trump signed a new federal spending bill. The bill detailed US spending for defense, security, healthcare, and more. Gun control was included in the bill. It promised funds to strengthen background checks and improve school safety across the country.

Changing gun policy at both state and federal levels requires willing lawmakers. But not all lawmakers were happy to support tighter gun control. So, the Parkland survivors turned to the upcoming elections. They felt that if current lawmakers weren't willing to make changes, then it was time to vote in new representatives.

US presidential elections occur every four years. Congressional elections occur every two years. The congressional elections held between presidential elections are called midterm elections. This is because they occur halfway through a president's four-year term.

The 2018 elections were midterms. The Parkland survivors made these midterm elections a key focus of their campaign. One of their goals was to get more gun control supporters elected to Congress. They encouraged young, first-time voters to register to vote. The organizers hoped young voters would be more likely to vote for candidates who favored stricter gun control. The push for young people to vote was successful. Ten percent more people aged 18 to 29 voted in the 2018 midterms than in the 2014 midterms.

Polls have shown that most US citizens support limits and regulations concerning gun ownership and use. However, opinions about gun control are often influenced by the political party a person identifies with. In the US, Republicans and Democrats represent the two dominant political parties. Most political candidates belong to one of these two parties.

Republicans are more likely to fight for the right to own and use guns. Many Republicans maintain that guns are not the problem. They believe the problem is the criminals who use guns. Tightening gun control, these Republicans argue, will not stop criminals from causing harm. Democrats generally believe the opposite. They argue that if guns were harder to get, fewer people would be harmed or killed by criminals.

The Parkland students expressed their anger over lawmakers' inability to make progress. In an interview on CNN, activist David Hogg addressed the nation's politicians. He told them, "You need to take some action and play a role. Work together. Come over your politics and get something done."

On March 14, the NRA posted a meme of a gun on social media. It was captioned, "I'll control my own guns, thank you." Later that day, the #NeverAgain team posted a response. It included a picture of young people protesting. They captioned the picture, "We'll control our own lives, thank you."

Hogg was frequently interviewed by the media and had nearly one million followers on Twitter in 2019. He used these platforms to share his opinions about politics and gun reform.

Money adds another layer to the complex political divide over gun control. Politicians need money to campaign and make their views known. So, people who support a particular politician or political party can donate money to help their campaign.

One organization that donates money to politicians is the National Rifle Association (NRA). The NRA was founded in 1871. It was started by former members of the military to improve troops' shooting skills. Since then, the NRA has grown in size and influence. According to the NRA's website, there were 5 million members in 2018.

The NRA is a national leader in firearms training and education. It promotes firearm safety. NRA members also strongly believe in a person's right to own and use a gun.

The NRA donates millions of dollars to political campaigns. Most of this money goes to Republican candidates. This is because more Republicans than Democrats agree with the NRA that gun control measures violate the US Constitution's Second Amendment. The NRA hopes those candidates, if elected, will oppose passing gun control laws. On the other side, groups such as Everytown for Gun Safety donate more money to Democratic candidates, who tend to support gun control.

Historically, gun control organizations have not donated as much to political campaigns as the NRA. So, candidates who favor gun control tended to receive less money from gun-related groups. During the 2016 election, the NRA and other gun rights organizations gave almost $55 million to candidates. Gun control advocates contributed only $3 million.

Gun control group Moms Demand Action for Gun Sense in America combined with Mayors Against Illegal Guns to form Everytown for Gun Safety.

However, this trend changed during the 2018 election. For the first time in many years, gun control groups donated more money to election campaigns than the NRA. This could be a hopeful sign for the #NeverAgain movement.

The Parkland shooting was not the first of its kind. But reaction to the tragedy was unique. Through the efforts of #NeverAgain, the Parkland shooting was a topic of national discussion for months. The 17 victims of the shooting became symbols of the fight to make America's schools safer.

The #NeverAgain movement breathed new life into the US gun control debate. Within weeks, #NeverAgain grew from a conversation in a student's living room to a nationwide discussion. The online presence of #NeverAgain spurred thousands of young people to march the streets to send a message to US lawmakers. And in their fight for policy change, youths of all backgrounds found common ground.

The long-term mission of #NeverAgain was to mobilize young voters nationwide. In this way, activists hoped, long-term change might be achieved. This mission

TAGGED

#NeverAgain never again will this happen in Parkland. Never again will it happen anywhere. Never again. Join the movement. Be the movement.
—#TurnoutTuesday
(@Turnout_Tuesday, Twitter)

AARON

HELENA RAMSAY

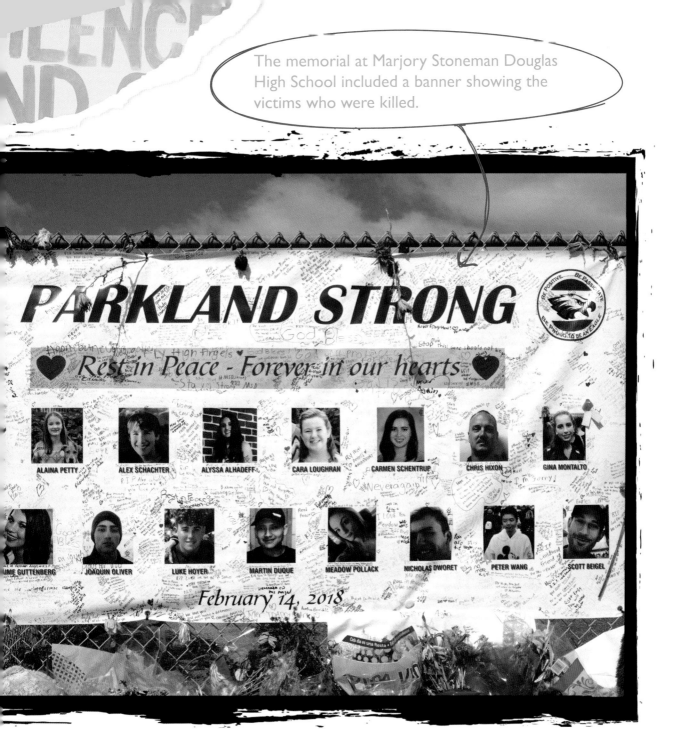

The memorial at Marjory Stoneman Douglas High School included a banner showing the victims who were killed.

was transformed by social media. The #NeverAgain founders showed how powerful a hashtag can be. And students who were not yet old enough to vote were suddenly leading a national conversation for change.

TIMELINE

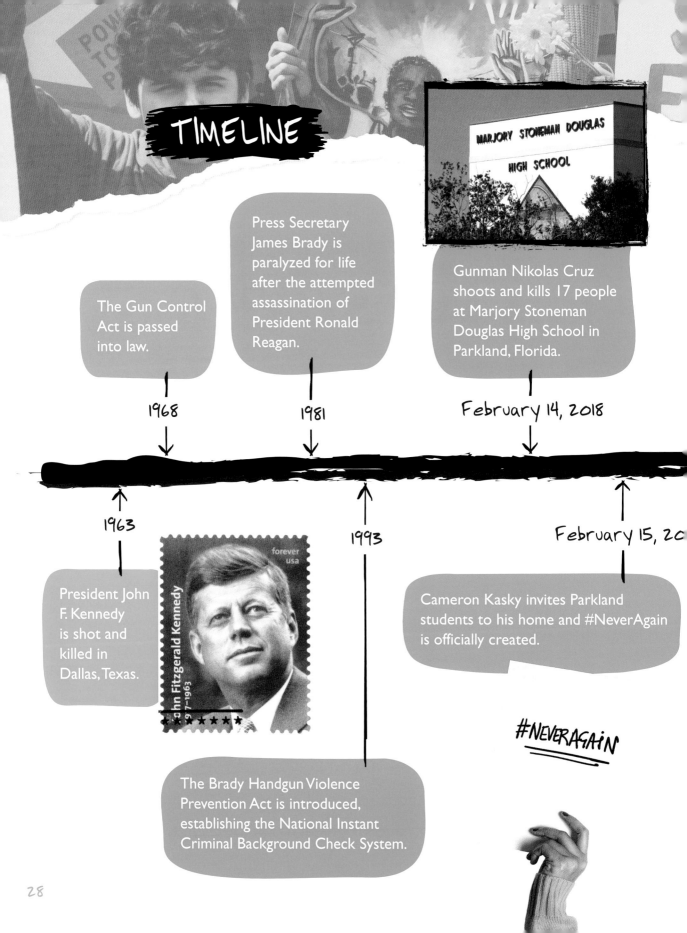

The Gun Control Act is passed into law.

Press Secretary James Brady is paralyzed for life after the attempted assassination of President Ronald Reagan.

Gunman Nikolas Cruz shoots and kills 17 people at Marjory Stoneman Douglas High School in Parkland, Florida.

1968

1981

February 14, 2018

1963

1993

February 15, 20

President John F. Kennedy is shot and killed in Dallas, Texas.

Cameron Kasky invites Parkland students to his home and #NeverAgain is officially created.

The Brady Handgun Violence Prevention Act is introduced, establishing the National Instant Criminal Background Check System.

#NEVERAGAIN

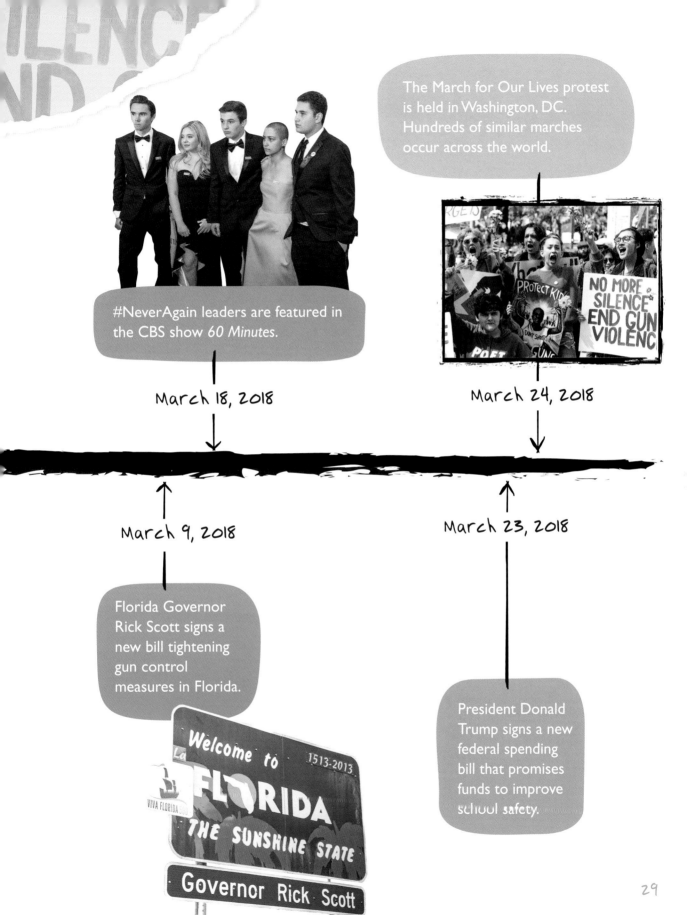

The March for Our Lives protest is held in Washington, DC. Hundreds of similar marches occur across the world.

#NeverAgain leaders are featured in the CBS show *60 Minutes*.

March 18, 2018

March 24, 2018

March 9, 2018

March 23, 2018

Florida Governor Rick Scott signs a new bill tightening gun control measures in Florida.

President Donald Trump signs a new federal spending bill that promises funds to improve school safety.

NO MORE SILENCE END GUN VIOLENC

PROTECT KID

Welcome to
La
FLORIDA
VIVA FLORIDA 500
1513-2013
THE SUNSHINE STATE
Governor Rick Scott

GLOSSARY

activist—a person who takes direct action in support of or in opposition to an issue that causes disagreement.

advocate—a person who defends or supports a cause.

amendment—a change to a country's or a state's constitution.

assassinate—to murder a very important person, usually for political reasons. Such an act is an assassination.

coordinator—someone who organizes people or groups to work together toward a common goal.

debate—a discussion or an argument.

Democrat—a member of the Democratic political party. Democrats believe in social change and strong government.

donate—to give. A donation is something that is given.

hashtag—a word or phrase used in social media posts, such as tweets, that starts with the symbol # and that briefly indicates what the post is about.

mainstream—the ideas, attitudes, activities or trends that are regarded as normal or dominant in society.

meme—a funny or interesting picture or video that spreads widely through social media.

militia—an army of citizens trained for emergencies and national defense.

monitor—to watch, keep track of, or oversee.

Republican—a member of the Republican political party. Republicans are conservative and believe in small government.

social media—websites or smartphone apps that provide information and entertainment and allow people to communicate with each other. Facebook and Twitter are examples of social media.

spotlight—public notice or attention.

traumatized—affected by extreme physical injury or emotional upset.

ONLINE RESOURCES

Booklinks
NONFICTION NETWORK
FREE! ONLINE NONFICTION RESOURCES

To learn more about #NeverAgain, please visit **abdobooklinks.com** or scan this QR code. These links are routinely monitored and updated to provide the most current information available.

INDEX